The Causes of Aggression

A Practical Approach

10

by

Vida Pearson

Sheffield
Hallam University

PAVIC Publications,
Sheffield Hallam Univ
36 Collegiate Crescen
Sheffield S10 2BP.
England

Tel 0742 532380.

Causes of Aggression

P52643-B3 (C)

Published by PAVIC Publications,
Sheffield Hallam University
36 Collegiate Crescent,
Sheffield S10 2BP.
England.

Tel 0742 532380.

Printed by Thomson-Stone Inc.
7300 West Joy Road, Dexter, Michigan, 48130, USA

First Edition 1993

Typesetting and graphics Jane Heaton
Cover by Freehand, Leicester

Edited by Shirley Payne
with thanks also to Manjeet Tara and Jackie Evans

ISBN 0 86339 3020

American Edition Distributed by
Inland Book Company
140 Commerce St
East Haven CT 06512
Tel (800) 243 - 0138

These words and their meaning are dedicated to

Balwant Kaur Panesar

and

Kiranjit Ahluwalia

Some History

The need for greater understanding of what the causes of aggression are is very apparent. There is much training and sharing of skills going on around the country, often initiated by women, on dealing with conflict and violence.

This 'boom' in interest has arisen as a direct result of many years of campaigning and struggling around issues of harassment, both in and outside the workplace. There is more likelihood now that a black person or woman will have their voice heard if they complain about aggression directed at them.

In this brave new world of equal opportunities, dealing with aggression must be taken very seriously indeed. Managers, trainers and equal opportunity specialists are becoming far more aware of the real concerns that staff face when dealing with aggression at work. The thinking in this document has emanated directly from the author's extensive experience in managing conflict.

Vida first worked in the Derry and Belfast communities in the very early '70's, in Ulster. She then lived and worked in inner city areas of Philadelphia, USA, for three years, where she also obtained her Masters Degree in Social Policy and Planning.

Following this she worked as a Neighbourhood Centre Organiser and then as a Sports Centre manager in Brent, London where she also lived. Her direct service delivery work has always been characterised by users of all races, ages, abilities or disabilities, income level and of either sex including lesbians or gay men, participating in activities designed to meet their requirements.

Her customers were respected in all their diversity as a matter of priority. Consequently, over the ten years of her responsibility for facilities, there was never any graffitti or vandalism and no physical abuse whatsoever. Emotional abuse was always defused by attending to the apparent needs of the customer first.

Much of the theory has been developed through working directly with women and particularly the women staff at Leicester Recreation and Arts Department where she was Womens Officer for two years. She was also a founding member of Brent Womens Aid.

WELCOME TO THE READER

This package is designed for managers, trainers and educationists who have responsibility for directing other people's thinking on issues around aggression. It has a layout designed for easy and accessible comprehension.

In this document you will find:

Definitions to clarify exactly what is meant by words which can be easily misconstrued.

Explanations which can lead the reader into making connections between concepts or which amplify ideas.

Examples which give some pictures and which can also allow the reader to think on their own.

Issues to help us question our assumptions of ourselves and each other, and what we do about them.

Time for you to think so that there is reason to pause and re-consider behaviour in the light of learning.

The purpose of this document is:

To provide practical insight into the causes of aggression which is concerned solely with DEFINING the terms we so often use - but which we have not, as yet, fully understood.

Using the materials

Remember to use this document alongside assertiveness training materials.
Recommended:
"Assertion Training"
by Deborah Clarke and Jacky Underwood
Effective Trainer Series
National Extension College
18 Brooklands Avenue
Cambridge CB2 2HN
England

CONTENTS

Causes of Aggression

Vida Pearson

The Causes Of Aggression
A Practical Approach

Introduction

**Staff who provide
Quality Customer Service
are equipped to
Deal with Aggression.**

One of the most worrying aspects of delivering a high quality customer service is knowing how best to deal with aggression when it arises.

As managers of people we are aware that aggression can occur in many forms. It is sometimes predictable and at other times it can happen unexpectedly, when you are least prepared for it. Every human being has the potential for aggressive behaviour and all of us will have experienced it in one form or another.

When preparing staff for their dealing with an aggressive customer we must ensure that their understanding of the situation allows them to make the correct decisions in how to tackle it. Unless we are familiar with the causes of aggression we will not be completely equipped in knowing how to cope. It is imperative that staff have some simple and straightforward guidelines to give them confidence in their decision making.

It is unfortunate that so much literature and thinking on violence has obscured what is actually very obvious. We all know about aggression because we can all become aggressive. If we understand first what makes US aggressive, then we are in a better position to manage both ourselves and the other person at the same time.

In this document we examine the issues in this sequence:

What is quality customer service?

What is aggression?

Manipulative or indirect aggression

Overt verbal aggression

Physical aggression

Harassment

Violence

What are the causes and context of aggression?

1 Fear

2 Humiliation

3 Frustration

What equipment should a staff member have when dealing with aggression?

1 Professional confidence

2 Comfortable environment

3 Good service

4 Satisfactory completion of activity

What are the dynamics involved between parties?

Issues of equality and power

What are the likely triggers of aggression or violence?

Individual

Organisational

Circumstantial

Further triggers

What are the responsibilities involved and to whom do they belong?

Management

Staff

The customer

Conclusion

The purpose here is to define plainly three causes of aggression so that individuals are able to recognise them. The hope is that this understanding in itself may prevent aggression before there is any hint of hostility.

After defining the causes of aggression we then examine the context within which hostility may arise. This is important because circumstances themselves can trigger an aggressive response. Common to all situations however, will be one, two or all three of the basic causes of aggression.

We do not go into any depth on HOW TO DEAL with aggression. Considering methods and techniques in this document would detract from the very first analysis of the situation.

What Is Quality Customer Service?

Quality customer service relies on these elements:

- A workforce which has self respect, feels in control and acts with professional confidence.

- An environment which offers the customer a reasonable sense of comfort and safety.

- The customer receiving a service which meets or exceeds their expectations.

- A satisfactory completion of activity which maintains the self esteem of all parties involved.

These four areas are integral to the fabric of the causes of aggression and will be returned to later.

What Is Aggression?

Aggression is a human emotion which compels the individual to act in either a defensive or offensive manner.

The action usually is perceived, by others, to be hostile in some way. Aggression often manifests as a very self-centred forcefulness which assumes superiority over another person or individuals.

Examples of aggressive behaviour are:

- **Manipulative or indirect aggression**

  Sulking, scowling, over-exaggerated body language, sarcasm, undermining humour, veiled threats, patronising, uncalled for comments, blaming, malicious gossip, using other people to hide behind, intentionally gaining personal goals at the expense of others.

- **Overt verbal aggression**

  Obscene language, 'in-crowd' jargon, offensive humour, bullying, growling, shouting, screaming, torrential speech, improper use of personal authority, demanding, accusing, warnings, open threats, 'winding-up', taunting, racist or sexist language, pompousness, over-complicated terminology, labelling, unfair criticism, inappropriately silencing others, unexpected outbursts, put-downs, attacking, retaliating, controlling.

- **Physical aggression**

  Thumping the table, pointing a finger, unexpectedly pushing back the chair, clenching fists, raising fists, moving too close, becoming too tense and erect, looking down 'from on high', hands on hips, one foot coming forward, leaning towards, blood pressure rising, punching the air, leering, staring, following, pacing up and down, withdrawing without notice.

  It is important to distinguish aggressive behaviour from two other actions of hostility, harassment and violence. Whereas both these behaviours rely on aggression they are actually extensions which are far more serious.

- **Harassment**

  This form of aggression is an undermining action which seeks to frighten and usually continues over a period of time.

  We are aware that racial and sexual harassment is a form of degrading black people and women and is used against them to keep them inferior.

  However, anyone might experience harassment if they are subjected to a bullying attitude by someone else who assumes a superior position.

  Harassment may take many forms which could include any of the above characteristics of aggression. But, it is its repetitive nature which distinguishes how serious it is.

- **Violence**

  The end result of aggression is the use of physical violence. Those who are violent will be expecting total submission of their victims. It is one of the ugliest forms of human behaviour and is completely unacceptable.

  Physical sexual harassment is violence - so any form of unwanted touch is a violence to the victim.

  Excessive verbal and emotional abuse can also be seen to be violent, if the result or intention is to subjugate the victim.

  Physical injury or damage is clear violence.

So, what then, are the causes of this behaviour? Why is it that some people will become aggressive, and others will remain thoroughly calm, even though the circumstances are the same? The action of aggression will have been *generated* by an emotion which has caused the individual to feel something very intensely.

He or she will have personally responded to circumstances with one, two or all of these emotions:

    Fear

    Humiliation

    Frustration

It is argued therefore that the cause of aggression is not the external situation but the human response to it.

This is NOT to suggest that aggression is always wrong. Sometimes, individuals MUST become aggressive to save themselves from a destructive influence. That will be an action of self-survival and can take many forms.

If, however, we understand the emotions behind our actions we are far more able to analyse the validity of our aggression. We can use the strength of our emotions to channel the desire to change the circumstances we are in. Before we can understand the aggression of others we must consider how we personally can become aggressive. This then puts us in a better position to decide how valid another person's aggression is.

Defining what is meant by fear, humiliation and frustration helps us to do this.

The Causes Of Aggression
1. Fear

Simply, fear is a response to a believed threat. It stimulates the whole body to behave in a defensive, or offensive manner.

If fear is an alert system to tell us something is or may be wrong the healthy reaction to it is to do something about it.

> **It is commonly understood that our natural response to fear is to:**
>
> **freeze**
>
> **take flight**
>
> **or fight**

The hormone adrenalin is pumped rapidly around the body when we are under threat and activates everything. Mind and muscle take over and select maybe one of the above reactions. In a serious situation you may not feel at all in control.

Suddenly, this 'other' person comes out and you may find yourself frozen to the ground (when you thought you'd always fight). Alternatively, you may find superhuman powers like the mother who somehow manages to lift a car off her child after an accident.

Freezing

Fear is a monumental surge of energy running through you which can electrify and warn you. The freezing action may be a way of preventing you from moving because to move may be the wrong thing to do.

- Knowing there is a burglar inside the house as you stand stuck on the doorstep unable to move is an example of frozen fear.

- Completely blanking-out when the police officer asks for your name and address after stopping you, is also a fear reaction of freezing.

Flight

Taking flight is an escape mechanism which responds to the fear by acknowledging how serious it is and urges you to get away from the threat.

- Running away from a street mugger is an obvious reaction to the fear you are feeling.

- Making an appointment with the dentist, going on the bus and then turning around and returning back home is also an example of reacting to fear.

Fight

Fighting is a strongly aggressive reaction to fear and is a common response. It is a means of overcoming that which is causing fear. There is an attempt, through fighting, to stop the reason for feeling fear.

If a person threatens you and you are afraid for your life you may want to respond in a self defensive manner and try to prevent injury through injuring the attacker first.

Often, however it is not as clearcut as that. We may want to fight someone just because they look frightening. Or, we are afraid they will offend us in some way or other.

All the examples of aggression above illustrate the many forms fighting can take.

- The junior staff member who can't stop talking when in supervision may be afraid you are not listening to them.

- The colleague who gossips about others all the time may be afraid that they are being talked about.

- The team member who suddenly withdraws from a meeting with a great flourish and with no stated reason may be afraid of being 'put on the spot' by the team.

Fear provides the body with a physical reaction. The hormones rushing through the blood stream are pumped into the muscles and they are instantly prepared for what comes next.

Recognising that someone is fearful is part of understanding and recognising the early alarm signals of aggression.

Some of these are:

- Raised blood pressure

- Pounding heart beat

- Sweating or going clammy

- Shaking, having weakened muscles

- Going weak at the knees

- Churning stomach or butterflies

- Dry mouth

- Feeling hot or cold

- Being unable to speak or talking too much

- Incoherence

- 'Blind rage', everything is tense

- Breathing too fast or too slow

It is also important to understand that our reactions to fear may change rapidly. So, one minute we may be feeling frozen solid and the next we have changed into a full-blooded attacker. Reactions to fear can be very predictable and the potential for aggression is always there regardless of initial freezing or flight feelings.

Why Do We Become Fearful -
A Definition

*Fear arises because we register a **threat** to ourselves of:*

- *personal damage, injury or discomfort*

- *losing or not gaining the satisfaction of a basic human need*

- *losing or not gaining a privilege*

A threat *is something which may be felt as the action is happening.*

So, somebody may be hitting us and we register the threat, the fear and the expectation of a continued threat, all at the same time.

On the other hand we may feel a threat of something which may or may not happen, only that there is a risk of it happening in the future. This can be just as motivating as if it were to happen definitely. We will still feel fear because we are preparing for an eventuality and our body is getting ready for it.

> **The threat initiates the fear response.**

Threat of personal damage, injury or discomfort

The fear of personal damage is a fundamental fear common to everyone.

Damage may be anything from pure physical violence to mental damage which scores into our emotional well-being.

Injury is a further description of damage and implies some breakdown of physical or mental functioning. An injury needs to be mended if possible, otherwise we live with some sort of permanent damage which may have to be adjusted to.

Discomfort can be either physical or mental also, but is not necessarily life threatening. It is uncomfortable to be restricted in one's diet by rationing, but so long as the main elements of nourishment are there we will continue to survive.

- Physically, it is uncomfortable to have only a little water available to us so that we cannot have a bath each day. However, there is enough to wash in.

- Emotionally, we can feel discomfort when a relationship is not going the way we want it to.

It is important to distinguish these three areas because it allows us to put a matter of degree to our analysis of what we are afraid of.

Damage, injury and discomfort can be administered in these ways:

by other people

by the environment we are in

by ourselves.

Thinking time

Consider how you **respond** when you are under threat.

What sort of **symptoms** do you feel when you are afraid?

What symptoms have you seen in **other people** when they are afraid?

How do you **react** when you are frightened of being injured? If you believed somebody was about to injure you - how would you behave?

What makes you feel **uncomfortable** in life and how do you react?

Threat of losing the satisfaction of a basic human need.

We may feel a tremendous amount of fear if we were told that we would lose our home in the next week. The satisfaction of a basic human need is something which we all understand because we all have to survive.

There are needs which are common to all people:

The need for:

     Health

     Shelter

     Food

     Clothing

     Mobility

     Other people

If any or all of these areas are threatened we will feel fear of losing them. Our response to that fear may be one of defensiveness:

"I will not let anyone or anything take this away from me, I will fight".

Much aggression in this world is caused by the natural human response to this type of threat.

It is customary to want to defend one's livelihood, lifestyle and standard of living. It is the substance of war between nations at one extreme and anger at the Housing Department Office at the other. Being denied adequate housing will be a threatening and frightening experience. The individual may respond to their fear with anger and become aggressive.

The Housing Officer then has to manage:

    a. The practical circumstances of the individual's housing plight.

    b. The fear of the individual about how they will cope in the future.

    c. The ensuing aggression that may well be directed against the Housing Officer.

Questions for the professional service provider are however:

- Is my service fundamental to the satisfaction of human need?

- Does my customer also believe this?

- Am I ever in the position of altering or denying allocation of resources around basic human needs?

It is evident that staff working in the human services are always dealing with the satisfaction of human need. It is little wonder that so much aggression occurs in Social Security Offices since the allocation of money enables individuals to satisfy a number of basic human needs. It is imperative that staff have a sensitive and clear understanding of how their customers are feeling where this is concerned.

We do all interpret 'basic human need' in different ways and it may be that we can overlook what that means to customers when we are not ourselves experiencing any threat.

- The threat of removal of children from a parent can provoke tremendous fear in her. She may then respond defensively and aggressively.

  It may be that a social worker has not informed the parent that there is NO such threat, only assumed that the parent would know. A client's defensiveness may be based therefore, on lack of information.

The purpose of drawing out the element of basic human need is to alert staff members' professional sensitivity around what IS a basic human need.

- Food is basic to all residential settings. Its quality of provision may be very important to the residents because it is one of the few sources of pleasure to them. A change in the menu may cause aggression amongst residents because they have come to depend on that enjoyment as basic to their present living circumstances. Understanding that will help staff in making changes carefully.

Thinking time

What are my personal human needs?

How do I respond when any of them are threatened?

Would I react aggressively if my children were taken from me, or my house, or my job?

Threat of losing a privilege

These personal questions then bring us to considering what the difference is between satisfaction of a need and satisfying a desire for something which is superfluous to need.

This is defined here as a privilege.

A privilege is anything which we have access to using or owning which is over and above our basic survival needs.

It is not basic to our survival that we spend a large amount of money on an expensive car. Nor £100 for a meal out for two.

> **However, our reaction to the thought of our losing our income or lowering our income may well be one of fear. Because we may lose our high income we may be afraid of losing privileges that we have become familiar with. We may have to settle for a smaller car or no car at all. We may have to adjust to only eating at home.**

It is essential for the caring professional to understand the difference between human need and privilege. There are no clearly defined lines of demarcation. We are so used to receiving privileges in this society that we confuse them with needs. What is *necessary* is that we understand the human reaction to the fear of losing a privilege. It may be as strong as any other fear and can cause the individual to react extremely powerfully against the person or people who may be seen to be threatening them.

Thinking about our own privileges starts the process of understanding others and managing their responses.

Thinking time

Make a list of the privileges you have in your life which you might fear losing.

Make a list of the bare necessities on which you can survive.

Now consider which parts of your life you would defend against others taking them from you.

Providing A Fear-free Customer Service

Reminders on keeping customers feeling safe:

Physical surroundings:

- Approach to building is open, well lit, paths in good repair, public transport signposted.

- Buildings warm, well ventilated, well lit, welcoming decoration, good sign posting, easily accessible, noise is at acceptable levels.

- Furnishings comfortable and in good repair, health and safety concerns immediately attended to, sensitivity in design for those who are phobic in lifts or with heights.

Staff:

- Are able to reduce anxieties.

- Aware of how they may personally cause a threat and in what way.

- Understand their power if they are in a position of allocating or denying resources.

- Are able to calm and reassure someone who is frightened.

The Causes Of Aggression
2. Humiliation

Feeling humiliated can provoke some of the same physical reactions in us that fear can. However, the difference is that we are often left bewildered by the experience and it somehow feels like we have become *diminished*. This sense of becoming smaller can result in a deep contraction of the body physically and will have similarities with the freezing effect of fear.

However, 'coming to' from the bewilderment may result in losing the confusion and realising that an injustice has taken place. That will then provide a reason for a surge of anger which will be associated with wanting to fight. This therefore is a second cause of aggression. Once again, we all know how it feels to have been humiliated.

Why Do We Feel Humiliated -
A Definition

We can feel humiliation because circumstances have compelled a self-appraisal which prompts us to feel inferior through:

> *- being made to feel "less than we thought we were or should be" (often through labelling or stereotyping)*

> *- being treated with disrespect to our own personhood*

> *- being treated unfairly or with injustice*

Feeling less than we thought we were or should be

It is an unfortunate aspect of this society that labelling and stereotyping are so much part of everyday life. Labelling gives attributes to an individual which are not necessarily at all accurate or even worse, are designed to make that person feel second-rate.

- Labelling all black people as 'immigrants' is not only to make a grossly inaccurate statement but also to suggest their second-class citizenship.

- Being 'only' a housewife or 'only' a secretary is to suggest in the description of the occupation that it is an inferior one to other occupations - husband or manager. It therefore further suggests that the housewife and secretary are themselves inferior.

Often labelling relies on some physical characteristic which is drawn out as a means of illustrating the innate inadequacy of the person in question.

- People are said to be 'queer' if they 'look queer'. In other words they behave or dress differently from accepted heterosexual behaviour.

- The actual intention is to make gay or lesbian people feel less than 'normal' human beings and categorise them along with many other thousands and thousands of homosexual men and lesbians.

There is always an implication when people are labelled and stereotyped that they are not full human beings. These wrongs permeate our lives every day and we label others without even thinking.

"She's a woman so she can't mend that car".

"He'll never know how to cook the dinner".

"Without the correct accent you'll never get that job".

If we have unthinkingly or intentionally labelled another person we may cause them to feel aggressive in return. No one likes to be stereotyped and some people may flare up at the slightest hint of it.

Thinking time

What labels have made you feel diminished?

What would you become angry with now if someone were to label you?

When did you last label or stereotype someone?

What labels or stereotypes have you used lately?

Being treated with disrespect to our own personhood

When we are disrespectful we assume that another person is not worthy of our time, consideration or courtesy.

We expect the other person to be already inferior - even without labelling them first. We do not see them as important people, as we are ourselves, and we do not expect them to have the same rights as ourselves.

Being disrespectful towards others is either to:

Expect them to be invisible

Or, expect them to serve us in some way or other regardless of how we are behaving

In both cases the personhood of the other individual will be ignored. The full person is not recognised and they are assumed to be powerless and under our control. It is little wonder that this form of discourtesy can be a cause of aggression in the other person. It is intensely humiliating to be made to feel as if one is 'not there'. So too if someone should automatically expect to be served in spite of how offensively they are behaving.

If we have been made to feel invisible one way of reclaiming visibility is to become aggressive. The intensely humiliating feeling of inferiority may then be relieved because we are bringing back our own sense of ourselves as full human beings.

Being treated with disrespect can make us feel very angry and therefore we may want to hit back.

Thinking time

When have you been treated with disrespect, and by whom?

Have you seen others treated with disrespect? When?

When have you made other people feel invisible?

When do you expect others to serve you - regardless of how you are behaving?

Being treated unfairly or with injustice

We can all recall the occasion when we have been accused of lying and we were innocent. It makes us feel deeply humiliated and we can often end up doubting our own reality. A *false* accusation is an injustice and unless we can right the wrong we will still smart from it for some while.

Most of us would agree that treating anyone unfairly is wrong and yet it happens all the time. Sometimes it is done without thinking, like the teacher who constantly encourages the brightest children whilst ignoring the needs of the slower ones. Or it can be methodically instigated by those who wish to restrict others - like the racist employer who never hires black people, even though some are amply qualified.

An injustice occurs when someone is able to make a decision about another person which is founded on *biased* information. Usually the decision will have an effect on the individual and it is often punishing, for example:

- It is an injustice if a black person is put in prison for a fraud while for the same offence a white person is merely fined.

- It is an injustice if a man is given a suspended sentence for battering his wife and she continues to live in fear of the same crime occurring again.

When we consider service delivery we are aware that we must treat all our customers fairly and with the same spirit of justice. It is no good giving some customers more of our time than others whom we feel may not be worthy of our attention for some reason or other.

If a customer feels as if they have been unfairly treated they may well turn to an aggressive behaviour in order to express their disgust at being so treated.

Thinking time

Think of an incident when you were unfairly treated.

What do you feel when you have been unfairly treated?

Write a sentence or two which says what injustice means to you.

Do you think others would agree with you?

What sort of situations do you find yourself in when you have the power to make decisions about or for other people?

How can you check on how fair you are being?

The humiliated customer is not a happy person so whereas the staff member may feel that they 'should not be there' the customer may turn aggressively against the staff member and make their presence felt.

It is imperative therefore that the customer feels:

- wanted

- openly received without prejudice

- treated with respect and courtesy

- given many opportunities to be treated with fairness and an appeal system available if they feel an injustice has occurred.

Causes Of Aggression
3. Frustration

Frustration can rise in us like a gush of hot water or a volcano about to blow or the proverbial steam coming out of our ears.

All our pent-up energies can feel as if they are going to explode and the commonest reaction is to become aggressive. We can also internalise the emotion and turn our aggression against ourselves. We can adopt self destructive habits such as blaming ourselves for everything that goes wrong.

However, the release of frustrated energy is often associated with an impatient outburst of some sort. At the bottom line though, is the feeling of not getting something that you want.

It is very important therefore, to distinguish what the want is.

Why Do We Become Frustrated - A Definition

Frustration can arise because of an impediment which provides a 'reason' for:

> *- a TANTRUM (which is a result of a loss or denial of a privilege) ie. Not getting what you want.*

> *- VALID anger or emotion at not having or getting something basic to human need.*

A tantrum

How many times do we stand in the queue wanting to hit something or someone because it seems we will never be served?

As adults we are not so very different from the two year old stamping, screaming and throwing ourselves on the floor. The *feelings* are the same. What we do about the feelings will be rather more sophisticated.

Or will it?

- The man whose sexual advances have been refused by a woman and then goes on to rape her, will be acting on the feelings of frustration which are based in a tantrum. He, quite simply, did not get his gratification first time round so he turns his frustration into violent aggression. The result is also to humiliate the woman and subjugate her.

- The child who consistently disobeys our instructions to do their homework will frustrate us and a smack will relieve that feeling and possibly force the child to do the homework.

- The neighbour who kicks next door's cat because it is crossing her lawn will have reacted to her frustration with a tantrum.

Mostly, we have a lot of good reasons for feeling frustrated:

"I have to get some other shopping as well as stand in this queue".

"That person is just not listening to what I have to say and I am more important than they are".

"You've just broken the TV and I can't relax without it".

Our expression of anger when indulging in a tantrum can be very fierce. It is a forceful extension of ourselves into the environment and upon other people. It is always about not getting what we want, when we want and how we want it.

It might be said that any act of belligerence against another person or people which is *unwarranted* is actually an expression of plain and unadulterated tantrum frustration. It is an unacceptable human behaviour and yet our society is designed for us to feel frustration quite often.

> **It is a regrettable fact of life that those who shout loudest often get what they want quickest.**

Our customer service must attend to this human reaction and protect staff and other customers from those who may wish to 'throw a tantrum'.

Valid frustration

Like the definition of fear we can also distinguish frustration as having VALIDITY at times. With all our reasons for feeling frustration we nearly always believe our frustration to be valid, worthy of us and those around us.

We will believe that we have a RIGHT to feel frustrated.

It is necessary to take an honest look at our lives and question what really *is* valid and what is a tantrum. Once we have distinguished in ourselves, the difference, we are in a better place to analyse our customers' frustrations.

It is argued that a valid frustration is one which is related to our basic human needs not being satisfied.

- It is valid to feel frustrated when we have not received our Social Security book and the children are hungry.

- It is valid frustration when we are angry when we realise that our young black children are being bullied at school and teachers will not listen or take action.

- It is valid to feel frustrated when the house we are renting has a leaking roof and the owner will not mend it.

- We can feel valid frustration when a doctor gives uncaring advice and leaves us with no assistance when we are in need of good medical help.

- It is valid to feel frustrated when your manager 'changes the rules' so that you cannot do the job you were employed to do.

When we provide a quality customer service we need therefore to be aware of how frustration, whether valid or a tantrum, can be a cause of aggression. The important issue is how the customer views the service and how much they feel that they rely on it in their lives. The point is that the professional service provider will wish to prevent any form of frustration arising since one unhappy customer will usually make many others unhappy too.

The caring professional will also be aware of what makes themselves personally frustrated and deal with that so that the customer is not having to handle their own frustration as well as the staff member's. Added to this, managers must ensure as much as possible that their staff are not feeling valid frustration in their work. Time and help should be given to staff to analyse what is valid and what is not.

Examples that can lead to valid work frustration:

- Being given poor professional direction and guidance

- Working in unhealthy conditions and managers ignoring staff concern

- Having shifts or breaks changed without good notice

- Not being listened to

- Not being given adequate training or guidance in dealing with 'difficult' customers.

- Changing working conditions without being consulted.

Examples of invalid frustration:

- Being impatient with elderly people who are not as quick as others

- Not wishing to take time to understand those who speak a different first language

- Expecting women colleagues to make tea

- Throwing equipment about the office because it has broken down.

Thinking time

Have a go at completing these sentences:

I throw a tantrum when ....

I have a right to feel frustrated when ....

When I am frustrated I feel so angry that I could ....

In what ways or situations have you the power to
make other people frustrated?

What Equipment Should A Staff Member Have When Dealing With Aggression?

Staff must feel equipped to deal with aggression so that they have confidence in their ability to reduce the risk of it occurring. There is an assumption here that management will constantly be striving to achieve the four components of providing quality customer service:

1.   A workforce which has self respect, feels in control and acts with professional confidence.

2.   An environment which offers the customer a reasonable sense of comfort and safety.

3.   The customer receiving a service which meets their expectations - or better.

4.   A satisfactory completion of activity which maintains the self esteem of all parties involved.

You will notice that each of the components refer implicitly to reducing the causes of aggression in all parties.

1. A workforce which has self respect, feels in control and acts with professional confidence.

Management will be working towards reducing any sense of humiliation amongst staff by encouraging an attitude of respect between colleagues. Self respect is also promoted through individuals feeling in control and having confidence in what they are doing.

Frustration is also reduced if staff are confident in the systems with which they work. Feeling in control of their own area of responsibility allows a staff member the freedom to exercise their own ability to deal with any difficult situations that may arise.

Their abilities will rely on their having been equipped with:

- An understanding of the causes of aggression

- The correct training to do the job

- The knowledge of what their own personal style is and the encouragement to use it professionally

- A feeling of being comfortable with themselves and the part they play in the organisation ie. they are valuable.

- Professionally having knowledge of:

> - the service and what is offered as a whole
>
> - Codes of Practice which will protect them in the event of an emergency (where aggression is concerned)
>
> - what they are able to follow through themselves and when they have to 'hand over' to a senior officer
>
> - what resources are available to help them
>
> - understanding that there are different needs and expectations because of race, gender, sexual orientation, class, disability and age.

If staff are equipped with the above they will be far more likely to prevent aggression even arising in the customer. They will have a real sense of how aggression is caused and what to do if it does arise. However, they will be even further assisted if the workplace also provides the other three components:

2. An environment which offers the customer a reasonable sense of comfort and safety

If customers feel safe fear will be reduced and so will the likelihood of an individual feeling unnecessarily threatened. Feeling comfortable also helps to relax people and will reduce both anxiety - which is a form of fear - and frustration. A clean and friendly environment also conveys a welcome which reduces any risk of feeling humiliated by surroundings.

3. The customer receiving a service which meets their expectations or better.

Management must ensure that the service they advertise is the service they are providing. The customer should be clear about what they can reasonably expect from a service which in itself reduces frustration.

Expectations which are not met will frustrate and humiliate if someone is actively relying on a level of service. The experience can then create a feeling of fear in the individual when anticipating receiving the same poor service the next time.

This may then build a potent mix for future explosions.

4. A satisfactory completion of activity which maintains the self esteem of all parties involved.

Once the service has been provided all parties should feel satisfied that the best has been given. If everyone involved still feels their self esteem to be intact and healthy it lays strong foundations for future contact free of aggression.

What Are The Dynamics Involved Between Parties?

With all the above equipment to rely on a staff member should feel reasonably in control and in a position of legitimate authority with the customer.

There is still a DYNAMIC which should be understood however, so that the staff member is adequately protected in their dealing with the causes of aggression.

The customer can bring with them a sense of their own power which may be overbearing in the first instance. The customer may attempt to cause fear, humiliation or frustration in the staff member.

Staff should understand what this means - especially for instance if they are black, and are dealing with racist customers, or, they are women serving those men who see them only as sex objects or as inferior.

Management should be very aware of the issues and be unequivocal in their support of the staff member. Every effort should be made to prepare staff to deal with the customer themselves, but if there is any risk associated, management should be ready to assist.

Often however, a work environment which actively promotes equality and respect of individuals will be sufficient to keep overbearing customers in check. They will realise that the organisation treats everyone seriously, including themselves.

Reminders Of Triggers Which Can Cause Fear, Frustration Or Humiliation - And Consequently Aggression

Triggers may arise through something which is done because of:

- our attitude

- the kind of decisions we make and their effects

- the use of our power

- our sensitivity or lack of it

- the way in which we allocate resources

Something which the organisation does because of:

- bad policy

- poor management practice

- lack of resources

- the effect of the organisation on the individual

Something which is circumstantial:

- the interaction between people creating a dynamic for aggression to arise

- the past history which customers and staff bring to the situation

- the physical environment

- the mental state of mind that individuals are in and which they bring to the situation

- the physical pain which individuals may be silently experiencing

- the stress which individuals bring with them

- the cultural and racial differences between people

- the gender differences

- differences in ability

Further triggers

It is argued therefore that circumstances can act as triggers to aggression. In themselves, they are NOT the causes of aggression in an individual. The aggressive person is experiencing a disturbing emotion which prompts them to behave defensively or offensively. We will constantly wish to reduce the triggers that can set off these emotions.

We know that some people can keep perfectly relaxed when being personally abused or attacked.

Others however, will *respond* differently and want to fight back in return. Their feelings will be urging them to do this, while the relaxed person is keeping their own sense of control.

Reducing triggers helps prevent people *feeling* aggressive.

Once we have recognised this we are also in a better position to deal with more difficult situations - like those when people are under the influence of **alcohol** or **drugs** or **disturbed mentally.**

It is NOT **alcohol** which causes aggression. Many people do not become aggressive when they have had too much to drink. Alcohol lowers inhibitions because it physically depresses the nervous system. Therefore, any predisposition to easily feeling the emotions of aggression may be brought out indirectly by the relieving of those inhibitions.

The staff member dealing with a customer who is under the influence of alcohol must take even greater steps to prevent fear, humiliation or frustration in them. This will often feel like a very tall order but preventing violence is paramount and staff will need actively to support one another.

Drugs also do not cause aggression. All individuals react differently to drugs and it is useful to understand why this is:

i.   Each individual has their own personal expectation of how the drug will affect them, for instance, nicotine stimulates the body, but people often 'have a cigarette to calm down'.

ii. Each individual has their own personal history and make-up which affects how they respond to a drug.

iii. The situation the person is in will be interpreted uniquely by themselves.

iv. Society imposes restrictions and constraints on individuals which are punitive and to be feared.

The professional will need to understand these factors and once again be aware that causing fear, humiliation or frustration may quite easily trigger aggression.

The same should be said for those who are suffering **mental disturbance.** Treating people with respect at all times, talking to them patiently and with clarity will reduce humiliation and fear. Reassuring them about what can happen and what your role is in their future will help further to reduce fear. They may feel frustration because they are not in as much personal control as they would like to be. Patience in understanding their needs and concerns will always help.

In all three of these instances, reactions can be more easily provoked. However, the cause of aggression is the same for ALL people and those with dependencies or mental disturbance should not be labelled as being any different from ourselves just because their threshold of tolerance may be lowered.

What Are The Responsibilities And To Whom Do They Belong?

When providing a quality customer service we are interested in doing this without any aggression occurring at all.

> **The responsibility therefore is to:**
>
> **Prevent aggression**

Aggression should not take place:

Between managers and their personnel

Between colleagues

Between staff and customers

Between customers

ALL these people have certain responsibilities in preventing aggression.

Management

Managers have overall responsibility to:

- provide a situation for all four components of quality customer service to flourish (see page 45)

- equip staff with the necessary tools to prevent aggression

- reduce the likelihood of triggering fear, humiliation and frustration in both staff and customers

- have a personal understanding of the causes of aggression.

Staff

Staff have responsibility to:

- provide a quality customer service within the expectations of their job

- reduce the likelihood of causing fear, humiliation and frustration in customers

- have a personal understanding of the causes of aggression

- treat each other with respect.

The customer

The customer also has a responsibility to take part in the process of maintaining the self esteem of all parties involved.

It is not right if a customer takes advantage of their position to harass, intimidate or oppress a staff member or other customers. If the staff member is unable to contain the customer's aggression because they really are out to dominate, then it is right for the customer to understand what their responsibilities are.

Either the staff member or manager should feel entitled to point out to the customer that their dominating behaviour is wrong.

This, however, would be only done so long as staff and managers are sure that they have not been responsible for triggering aggression in the customer.

Conclusion

Aggression in today's society is part of every day life.

We all know how it feels to be aggressive and to feel another person's aggression.

The three causes of aggression are so simple as concepts that they can be easily understood by us all. Following this we can examine our own behaviour and that of others with far more comprehension. We can then make more informed decisions about how to proceed.

It is fundamental that if a staff member is unable to contain a situation they must either withdraw or obtain support. This is obvious common sense, but no one should feel so threatened that they are in real danger.

Keeping causes and triggers of aggression in mind both staff and the organisation can prevent any such occurrence.

Quality customer service will then be assured.

About Balwant Kaur Panesar

Balwant was killed by her husband, from whom she was hiding, in the Brent Womens Aid Refuge in London in 1985. At the precise time of her brutal murder, witnessed by her small daughters, the other women in the refuge were shouting from 1st floor windows at two police officers who were sitting in their patrol car outside.

The police dismissed the women as 'hysterical' and the murderer escaped.

About Kiranjit Ahluwalia

Kiranjit killed her husband after ten years of extreme violence and degradation by him against her. She believed her chances of surviving were rapidly diminishing. The evening before he had severely beaten her and pressed a hot iron against her face.

The prosecution in her case suggested she had 'only been beaten about a bit'.

Justice Leonard then convicted Kiranjit of murder and she was given life imprisonment at the end of 1989.

Southall Black Sisters successfully campaigned for her release in 1992. Please phone, London, 081 571 9595 for more details.

TRAINING AND CONSULTANCY

Vida Pearson is available to do training, consultancy or give advice around the issues raised.

Please write to:

**Pavic Publications,
Sheffield Hallam University,
36 Collegiate Cresent,
Sheffield S10 2BP
England**

Or phone 0664 434451

Notes